Oklahoma Summer

poems by

Margaret Lee

Finishing Line Press
Georgetown, Kentucky

Oklahoma Summer

Copyright © 2023 by Margaret Lee
ISBN 979-8-88838-109-0 First Edition
All rights reserved under International and Pan-American Copyright Conventions. No part of this book may be reproduced in any manner whatsoever without written permission from the publisher, except in the case of brief quotations embodied in critical articles and reviews.

ACKNOWLEDGMENTS

I owe special thanks to Paul E. Nelson and the Cascadia Poetics Lab for the annual Poetry Postcard Fest, for which I wrote early versions of "Flight Feathers," "The Center of the Universe," "Tulsa's Steel Bison," "Cain's Ballroom," "Blue Dome District," "Roadmap: Route 66," and "The Tavern." I send deep appreciation to the Society of the Muse of the Southwest (SOMOS) and its Executive Director, Jan Smith, for their excellent programs. I wrote "Displaced" for Veronica Golos's online SOMOS workshop, "Reading Deeply, Writing Deeply: Documentary Poetry." At the SOMOS 2021 Taos Writers Conference I wrote "Red Card" in Jeremy Paden's workshop, "Writing Alongside History" and "Contested Territory" in Juan Morales's workshop, "Writing the Poems of our Land."

The epigraph for "Prairie Garland" is in the public domain. The epigraph for "Three Springs Farm" comes from the *Three Springs Farm CSA Newsletter*, June 29, 2020. The epigraph for "Rest in Peace" comes from Joy Harjo, "Break My Heart," *An American Sunrise* (New York: W. W. Norton and Company, 2019) page 3.

Publisher: Leah Huete de Maines
Editor: Christen Kincaid
Cover Art: Margaret Lee
Author Photo: Bernard Brandon Scott
Cover Design: Elizabeth Maines McCleavy

Order online: www.finishinglinepress.com
also available on amazon.com

Author inquiries and mail orders:
Finishing Line Press
PO Box 1626
Georgetown, Kentucky 40324
USA

Table of Contents

Summer in Oklahoma 1

Prairie Profusion
Contested Territory 2
Immersion in Flint Hills 3
Prairie Garland 4
The Space Between 5
Saturday in Summer 6
Flight Feathers 7
Prairie Primrose 8
Sunflower Mirage 9
Oklahoma August 10

Tulsa Postcards
The Center of the Universe 11
Tulsa's Steel Bison 12
Cain's Ballroom 13
Blue Dome District 14
Three Springs Farm 15
The Tavern 17

Wounded
Roadmap: Route 66 18
Upon the Removal of a Tent from River Park near an Abandoned
    Least Tern Sanctuary on Memorial Day 19
Council Oak 20
Displaced 21
Red Card 22
Rest in Peace 24
The Mural 26

Rain and Drought
Spring Storm 27
Tulsa's Driest June on Record 28
Rain 29
When Bluestem Turns Red 30
Summer's End 31
Descent 32

*For Rick,
who carries Oklahoma
in his heart*

Summer in Oklahoma

Summer in Oklahoma always brings heat, storm, and explosions of life on the tallgrass prairie, one of the most severely threatened ecosystems on earth. In recent summers, human drama has eclipsed its natural wonders. A global pandemic, the likes of which the modern world had never envisioned, caught the state in a death grip, along with new moments of reckoning with Oklahoma's painful demographic history. Oklahoma's designation before statehood as Indian Territory for Native People who were forcibly removed from ancestral lands came home to roost on July 9, 2020. In an historic decision, the U. S. Supreme Court found that the reservation boundaries throughout eastern Oklahoma were never disestablished in the reconstruction treaties forged after the Civil War, reaffirming that the city of Tulsa and most of eastern Oklahoma rest on Indian reservations. Oklahoma's citizens now struggle to come to terms with the implications, amid intense opposition from the State government.

In the runup to the one-hundred-year anniversary of the Tulsa Race Massacre in 1921, long-unheeded cries to search for bodies rumored to be buried in mass, unmarked graves finally prompted the Tulsa City Council to act. In the summer of 2020, excavations began in Tulsa's Oaklawn Cemetery, where the remains of the massacre's victims were thought to lie. Forensic evidence remains forthcoming, and descendants of the massacre's victims remain unsatisfied. Meanwhile, the Black Lives Matter movement drew attention and backlash on the weekend of Tulsa's 2020 Juneteenth celebration, now a national holiday. A presidential visit for a re-election rally in 2020 was scheduled in Tulsa on the same weekend, during the pandemic. A street mural painted for these events along the former Black Wall Street became a flashpoint.

These poems register Oklahoma's summer heat. Even more, they celebrate Oklahoma's beauty, lament its people's pain, and reach for new possibilities.

Prairie Profusion

Contested Territory

Forbs and grasses crowd out the trees
along green ridges of tallgrass prairie.

A dickcissel calls. Scissortailed
flycatchers perch on power lines

at the generating station.
They scatter, then return

when a white pickup, caked
in red road dust, growls

along the gravel road at speed—
a race to the next pump jack,

moaning, creaking, weary
with the baking heat

its rhythmic movements
like the lumbering bison

across the road, their clouds of flies.
The rocky hills stretch out.

Prairie Profusion

Immersion in Flint Hills

I dive into grassy currents
over rolling prairie, swim
among schools of wildflowers—
goldenrod tendrils, clusters
of snow-on-the-mountain.
I bathe in their spreading
white blossoms, stabbed
with sharp green and spikes
of purple vervain, a floating
canopy of turkeyfoot seed heads.

A river of molten bronze
snakes toward the hill's crest
dark with shade—bison
in a narrow stream from high
on a scorched horizon—
this season's red calves,
brown yearlings with emergent horns
trail their mothers, noses to tails.
Bulls thick with flies shed clumps
of wooly winter shoulder blanket,
send up caramel clouds
from their dust wallows.

Above the verdant ocean
a swirling sky—
fleecy cloud-streaks
on blue-grey foundations,
distant thunderheads.
Wind scales the hills.
Blossoms bend, turn.

Birdsong breaks the quiet—
a meadowlark's whine
the bob white's two-note call,
a yellow-billed cuckoo's clatter—
no report— all swallowed
in rolling hills,
thick with blossoms
of yellow scurfy pea.

Prairie Profusion

Prairie Garland

> *Le lis que tu comprends, en toi s'épanouit.*
> *(The lily that you understand blooms within you.)*
> —Victor Hugo, Les Contemplations

Prairie—
buried rootwork
shelters its beating heart
in dark, silent variety
year long.

Color
awaits, deepens,
sends surges of lifeblood—
white at first—yucca and larkspur
burst like

popcorn,
dance, pirouette,
glowing like twinkle lights.
Then come blue and yellow clusters—
nightshade,

yellow
sweet clover, vetch,
prairie celestials—
churning color pulses, grassland
heartbeats—

orange
coreopsis,
butterfly weed—gold and
crimson blooms that set the prairie
ablaze.

Prairie
awaits, deepens,
glowing like twinkle lights
churning color pulses, grassland
ablaze.

The Space Between

the cicada meadow and scrub oak woods—
overgrown with weeds,
blackberries, poison ivy—
shelter for bob white quail,
wild turkeys, winter sparrows

Saturday in Summer

A clear, cool swim
breakfast in the garden
with coffee
birdsong
breeze…

Should I prune the bronze fennel?
Its blossoms fade yellow
on pale shoots
but their fragrance
stays strong.

No. Leave it
for the butterflies.

Flight Feathers

They drank their color
from the same paint pot—
Carolina wren, female
cardinal, rufous hummingbird,
the red-tailed hawk's
red tail.

Prairie Profusion

Prairie Primrose

Pink and pale, they erupt
where front-loaders gashed the ground
and graders raked the rocks.
Fragile flowers
atop slender stems
line the dirt roads,
their yellow centers beaming
innocence unabashed—
loveliness in profusion.
Their blossoms face the sun—
translucent, gratuitous—
like forgiveness.

Sunflower Mirage

A town
out west called Felt
on a secret mission
hidden on the Oklahoma
prairie

ignites
a brilliant fire
every year in July—
watered circles of sunflowers
dense, tall—

petals
school-bus yellow,
platens laden with seeds
on sturdy stalks with leafy green
streamers.

After
countless miles of
spent soil, resplendent blooms
engulf the visual field, loom
and blaze.

They last
just a moment.
As soon as they have drunk
the brutal summer sun, they die
cut down.

A town,
a brilliant fire—
platens laden with seeds
engulf the visual field, loom—
cut down.

Prairie Profusion

Oklahoma August

Butterfly weed and yellow coneflowers
mock the sun, send back its light
in yellow-orange fury.
The meadowlark's song defies the furnace.
A dickcissel calls, daring the clouds to rain.

Thistle heads explode in pink
as Prairie flaunts her verdant dress, sensuous
curves, sends up gauzy veils of bison-dust.
Let the heat blaze, she cries—
I was born in fire!

Tulsa Postcards

The Center of the Universe

We really call it that.
No sign or monument.
Just a circle of broken pavement
        on a bridge over railroad tracks
        in downtown Tulsa.
But if you stand there
        and whisper
your voice travels
        loud and clear.
I want to hear the five-year-old boy
        who only speaks Hmong.
The woman in the pink chenille jacket
        they just admitted to Parkside.
The chemist whose research
        remains unpublished.
Mr. Brewster, Tulsa county's tired
        public defender.
Our ancestors who walked here
        before there was a bridge—
let them speak from
        the center of our universe.

Tulsa Postcards

Tulsa's Steel Bison

Why place it on a street corner
        next to City Hall, emblazoned
        with the city's name?
Is it to remember
        what had been here,
        should be here?
Or to forget
        its nimble mass,
        fleecy shoulder blanket,
        its horn-daggers—
the fact that people
used to know
how to live with them
for real?

Tulsa Postcards

Cain's Ballroom

Neon star, silver disco ball
spins in a boom-and-bust town.
Built to shelter Tate Brady's cars
three years and one mile
from the Greenwood massacre—
ballroom home of Western Swing,
now the Old Lady on Brady—
parking lot closed to make way
for a pop culture museum—
contradiction in terms.
A city confused—
we only know
we need a place
to dance.

Tulsa Postcards

The Blue Dome

Dubious claim to fame—
Tulsa's first 24-hour gas station
when Route 66 ran along
Second Street downtown.

We named a whole district
for it, just because
someone built a dome
and painted it blue.

Tulsa Postcards

Three Springs Farm

> *From one year to the next, we can count on the cadence of the farm and find comfort in its promise.*
> —Emily Oakley and Michael Appel, Oaks, OK

Bitter with the bite
of February planting,
spiky arugula, tender tatsoi
come to harvest late in March
to be dressed with ginger,
orange slices.

April lettuces explode
in every green dimension:
white stalks, spreading blades
the color of limeade,
leaves curly, red-edged,
toothed and tendrilled filigree—
tiny, tender spinach leaves
on threadlike stems
then, soon, nubbly leaf-platters
wide as your palm,
green as grass at midnight.

    Effort and ease
    dip and dance
in ancient rhythm
    sowing and harvest
    working and watching
oscillation
    of rain and sun
    night and day,
measured pace.

May plantings
follow the leaf harvest.
Roots swell, earth bursts—
onions, white and red
    fragrant, green tops
    as long as your arm—

Tulsa Postcards

    patriotic potatoes in July,
            red, white, and blue—
    radishes crisp, bright.

    Then the summer color-swirl—
        broccoli and beets,
        turnips and tomatoes,
        cabbages, cauliflower,
        carrots—
each in due season
from soil wintered over
in oats, rye, daikon,
vetch and clover—
a waltz of toil and time
        wind and water
        air and earth.

Tulsa Postcards

The Tavern

He hears their voices
as he sits at a table
against the wall, alone—

the voices of those
who filled now-empty chairs
that scraped the floor

amid clinking glasses, laughter
explosions, the dull thud of dirty dishes
parked in plastic tubs.

He listens alone for echoes
of greetings, friendship slaps,
farewell hugs, and he remembers—

looks into the light from street-facing
windows, waits for a friend, a stranger—
any presence to ease the absence.

Wounded

Roadmap: Route 66

The Mother Road birthed
those green dinosaur gas station signs,
miles of dashed white lines,

single-story motor lodges.
Metro Diner in neon magenta promises
red vinyl seats, linoleum floors,

women in white aprons, peach-colored dresses—
clattering plates, coffee from bowling-ball pots
poured into carnival glass mugs.

The old black and white shield
says it's safe to get your kicks
in your Thunderbird.

The Mother Road divides her Tulsa children
north and south, black and white
like the map, like the postcard.

A pawn shop, a boarded-up grocery store
mark a strip mall on North Peoria.
The streets flood when it rains.

Under skies muddy with exhaust
another Mother maps her scars—
pavement ruptured by turbid streams

full of fertilizer, empty of fish— she traces
her different course across mountain and prairie
from Chicago to LA.

Upon the Removal of a Tent from River Park near an Abandoned Least Tern Sanctuary on Memorial Day

narrow asphalt trail—
from the ground up, I know it—
broken remembering place

> white streak—the call, crisp—
> three least terns, no landing place—
> aerial cursive

amid lush weeds
grey tent-dome on the sand spit
gone—no tent dweller

> cottonwoods let fall
> soft castanets of sky-breath—
> silver-backed leaf-hearts

WOUNDED

Council Oak

What is left of *Talasi*
lies behind a wrought iron fence—
limb clusters like many trees
from one deep-grooved trunk—
their destiny bent and twisted
like the clans who traveled here—
silent, tall, ancient, rooted
in sacred ground.

Tulsa encroaches—
this remade, renamed town.
A multi-story brick condo looms
to the north. To the south, 18th Street.
Toward the river to the west,
an apartment parking lot.
In between, a few feet
of close-clipped lawn.

The tree, full-grown
when they arrived, sheltered
ceremonial fire kindled from coals
carried across the Mississippi
to a new home on the Arkansas River.
Many-lobed leaves point
in all directions—today's compass—
fenced, silent.

Note: A wrought iron fence surrounds the Council Oak tree, a native white oak overlooking the Arkansas River. It marks the ceremonial grounds of the Muscogee (Creek) people who were removed from the southeastern United States and relocated to Indian Territory in 1836. The modern city of Tulsa takes its name from the Muscogee word, "*Talasi*," or "*Old Town*"—their designation for a home chosen for them by the U. S. government, then stripped away by allotment and Oklahoma statehood. For sixty years, the Muscogee people used the land surrounding the Council Oak for tribal business, feasts, and games until the land came under private ownership. When the titleholder decided in 1960 to fell the tree and pave the land for a parking lot, the Muscogee (Creek) Nation purchased the land, built a park around the tree, and donated it to the City of Tulsa. The park was placed on the National Register of Historic Places in 1992.

Displaced

My house sits
at the Crow Creek headwaters
in Tulsa, Oklahoma.
Since 1929 its faucets have drawn water
from lakes in Cherokee country.
Its drains send dishwater,
garbage, our toilet's contents
into sewers that snake
through Muscogee land.

Daily I drive on asphalt that smothers
diverted streams forced to hide
underground in conditions
they don't control.

Long before, Muscogee people—
driven from ancestral land—
fled to territory granted
by a promise, broken—
now paved, plotted,
scored by streets, power lines.

I cannot burn cedar branches,
fan the smoke
with eagle feathers,
blur the edge
of what I think of
as my home.
The Muscogee deities
do not speak to me,
for I do not know
their names.

We do not belong.

Note: On July 9, 2020, the U.S. Supreme Court decided in Oklahoma v. McGirt that the U.S. Congress never disestablished the Muscogee (Creek) Nation's reservation in its 1866 treaty that reduced native ownership rights to land in Indian Territory. Most of the city of Tulsa lies inside their reservation boundary. The tribe's legal jurisdiction in criminal prosecutions, which had been usurped by the State of Oklahoma since statehood in 1907, was restored by this historic Supreme Court decision.

Wounded

Red Card

Cotton. Money. Land.
    Existing treaties insufficient ...
A Georgia farmer lifted a Red Stick. Muscogee blood ran.
White settlers held their ground. Muscogee people ran.
Red card.

    Forfeit to the United States all benefits ...
Forced march. Barges. 21,792 Muscogee departed.
Twenty years later, they numbered 13,573—
the new Creek Nation in Indian Territory.
Red card.

    Whereas the Creeks made a treaty with the so-called Confederate States ...
    The United States require of the Creeks a portion of their land ...
    the west half of their entire domain.... thirty cents per acre ...
Slaveholding rebel states retained their land.
Red card.

    Their nation independent and self-sustaining.
Tribal courts abolished. Red card.
    United States guarantees them quiet possession of their country.
Tribal land ownership erased. Red card.
    Forever secure.
The former Creek Nation Reservation was disestablished at statehood. Red card.

    Reversed.

    Unlawful acts, performed long enough
    and with sufficient vigor,
    are never enough to amend the law.

Welcome to the Mvskogee Reservation.
    Forever set apart as a home
    As long as the rivers run.

The river runs through Tulsa—
    waters the Muscogee Council Oak
    flows past where a commission— all white—

met a native delegation armed
with banners, flags, and red cards.

The river runs three miles from my house.
Red card.

Note:
Words above in *italics* quote passages from the U. S. Treaty with the Creek Nation (June 14, 1866, Ratified July 19, 1866, Proclaimed Aug. 11, 1866), the U. S. Supreme Court decision in McGirt v. Oklahoma (July 9, 2020), and a banner displayed at a town hall meeting in Tulsa on July 13, 2021.

Oklahoma's governor, Kevin Stitt, called the meeting to discuss implementation of the McGirt decision. The governor appointed no Native people to his commission, nor did he invite the chief of the Muscogee (Creek) Nation to the town hall meeting. When the governor's representatives arrived, they were met by a group of Native People carrying the flag of the American Indian Movement and a banner that read, "Welcome to the Mvskokee Reservation." Native People crowded the meeting room. Since they were not invited to speak, they instead raised red cards each time the governor or a commission member made an inaccurate or offensive statement. This occurred so frequently that the governor disbanded the meeting. (https://tulsaworld.com/eedition/page-a1/page_4859b409-fcd9-518f-b56b-9c5f9c11e703.html)

Wounded

Rest in Peace

> *There are always flowers,*
> *Love cries, or blood.*
> —Joy Harjo, "Break my Heart"

A lone bouquet
        tender pink-petaled blossoms
        and purple flower-spikes
        in a leafy nest, swaddled
        in crumpled brown paper
rests
near a freshly dug pit
at Oaklawn cemetery
where they search
for mass graves.

No one knows, really;
Really?
Surely someone … someone …
There is only unrest
for the searchers
        who disturb graves
        of those properly entombed
only unrest
for all who waited
        almost a hundred years
        since the streets burned
when choking smoke
        hid the horror
        forced folks to flee—
dead bodies in the street.

Hushed rumors whisper
there … there …
there lies my uncle,
neighbor
barber
grandfather
mechanic …
Seeking truth at last

Wounded

they dig today
>to face it full
>hear the silent rebuke
>of innocent dead.

But in the pit
they find
unrest.

We still don't know, really;
Really?
Surely someone ... someone ...
someone carried the bouquet
to the pit's brink—
eternal rest
>for the unknown
>for what will come
>for what we will learn.

Note:
On June 1, 1921, an armed, white mob stormed Black Wall Street in Tulsa, Oklahoma and burned it down in the infamous Tulsa Race Massacre. Since then, many have claimed that uncounted victims of the massacre were buried in unmarked, mass graves in Tulsa's Oaklawn Cemetery. On July 13, 2020, city officials, municipal workers, anthropologists, and archaeologists began to excavate the cemetery in search of mass graves from the 1921 massacre. The following day, a newspaper photographer captured the image of a bouquet of flowers lying at the rim of the excavation site. (https://tulsaworld.com/news/local/test-excavations-in-tulsa-race-massacre-mass-graves-search-resume-monday/article_e9ce3502-9923-5d24-916f-b481cfb47a59.html#5)

Wounded

The Mural

Tulsa wept in black and white
because of black and white
until the streets ran red
with blood.

Now weeping in color
because of color
the street glows
with yellow paint.

Three bright words
in bold, straight lines,
a Greenwood gift—
proud fist just in time.

Dark deed
a drive-by blue slash
again, tears
more yellow paint.

Note:
Tulsa was selected as the location for the first campaign rally for then-president Donald Trump since the onset of a global pandemic. The rally was scheduled for the weekend of June 19, 2020, "Juneteenth," the nationally commemorated celebration of the end of slavery in the U. S., now a national holiday. In recognition of the anniversary and in preparation for the president's arrival, a local artist and a community of supporters painted "Black Lives Matter" in yellow block letters on Greenwood Avenue where Tulsa's Black Wall Street was burned to the ground in the 1921 Tulsa Race Massacre. Several weeks later, an unknown person defaced the mural during the night, drawing a thin line of blue paint through the words. The following day, community members repainted the mural.
(https://tulsaworld.com/black-lives-matter-sign-in-tulsa-defaced-with-blue-paint/article_73f43fb8-d7ec-516e-9ddd-c8cf3649f13f.html)

Rain and Drought

Spring Storm

It's thundering again—
a remote rumble
like the muffled sound
from an upstairs bedroom
after a houseguest
awakens from a nap—
a warm, welcome guest,
your grandfather maybe—
someone whose noises
you understand.

You know what he is doing
and what will happen next.
No need to look out the window
watch the radar
check for storm warnings.
I just listen, pleased
that my guest has come,
knowing how it will be
when he is gone,
ready to receive
the coming rain,
waiting for it,
not wanting to change it
or take shelter.

The quiet rumbling
brings his presence close
wraps me in grey
makes the rain inevitable
starts a familiar cycle
like boarding the school bus.
You know the route,
the destination,
the agenda when you arrive.

And now the rain.
Peace.

Rain and Drought

Tulsa's Driest June on Record

Spent fennel blossoms—brittle,
yellow, cloaked in lingering
licorice perfume—despair
of rain. Englemann's daisy
lies a sapless heap across
the sidewalk, its stems and leaves
a tangled mass. Betting on
survival, it redirects
its energy to the bees
on its once-cheerful blossoms
before they shrivel and fade.

Not having bloomed this season,
patches of brown-eyed Susan
resign themselves to their roots
to try again next summer.
Even purple coneflowers
droop. Wilting petals hang limp
like a cropped coiffe spoiled by rain;
except that there is no rain.

Heavy flowerheads incline
their stems, all leaning as if
straining to hear some muffled
conversation, or rumors
of rain; rain that never comes.

Rain

The day's first sound—
both a pressure
and its release—
rain.
Not a pummeling storm
or windy assault
but homogenized sound—
drops on window-glass
drape like a single veil—
a general noise
unique quiet.

For a moment
everything stops.
Only the rain exists.
And you know
if you looked out
it would be heavy, grey—
a slick patina
weighing everything down—
the weight a relief,
reassuring.

Tree limbs receive the dousing.
Grass waits for the water
to reach its roots.
I, too, begin to open
as the quiet settles in,
as the water reaches
my roots.

Rain and Drought

When Bluestem Turns Red

Bluestem
half-moon seed heads
curl on the rusty blade,
arch their spines, throw back their wispy
white husks

as if
laughing, dancing—
as if their fuzzy tufts
embrace their coming dormancy
unfurled.

Summer's End

August—
packed earth, baked ground
pinches stems, shrivels leaves,
chokes color from coreopsis—
hot, tired.

Almost
like despair, like
the earth's final effort,
nearly forgetting roots growing
deeper.

Rain and Drought

Descent

Acorns
tap the asphalt
when they fall, but landing
in the soft grass they are silent,
hidden.

That fall
beckons, invites
an imagined descent
into the fecund, verdant earth
unheard,

unseen.
I could lie there
for days, invisible
sheltered by the grass, the tree's shade,
darkness

until
my shell would crack,
give way to insects, rain,
a squirrel's teeth—a tender sprout with
new roots.

Margaret Lee is a poet, fiber artist, watercolor sketcher, aspiring naturalist, and scholar of the ancient world. Her debut poetry collection, *Someone Else's Earth* (Finishing Line Press, 2021), contains poems inspired by fragments of the ancient Greek poet, Sappho. Her second chapbook, *Sagebrush Songs* (Finishing Line Press, 2022), meditates on landscapes of northern New Mexico.

Margaret is retired as Assistant Professor of Humanities at Tulsa Community College in Tulsa, Oklahoma. She attended Edgecliff College in Cincinnati, Ohio and graduated with a Bachelor of Arts in History from Seattle University in Seattle, Washington. She earned a Master of Divinity degree from Phillips Theological Seminary in Tulsa, Oklahoma, and a Doctor of Theology degree from the Melbourne College of Divinity in Melbourne, Australia. She edited *Sound Matters: New Testament Studies in Sound Mapping* (Eugene, OR: Wipf and Stock, 2018) and co-authored *Sound Mapping the New Testament* (Salem, OR: Polebridge Press, 2009) with Bernard Brandon Scott. Margaret has written numerous articles on the Greek language and New Testament studies in edited books and peer-reviewed academic journals.

Margaret worked in the finance industry in Seattle for six years, then twenty-five years in higher education in Tulsa as a faculty member and administrator. She raised her daughter and son in Oklahoma and now has three grandchildren. Margaret avidly pursues the fiber arts, including spinning, weaving, and knitting. She enjoys sketching with pencil, ink, and watercolor. Margaret is an enthusiastic birdwatcher. She loves exploring the Oklahoma prairies, New Mexico deserts, and Oregon coastal forests and seashores. Margaret is a member of the Society of Biblical Literature and a fellow of the Westar Institute. She has served as an officer of the Tulsa Handspinner's Guild and the Tulsa Handweavers Guild. Margaret is a member of the Tulsa NightWriters, the Oklahoma Writers Federation, Inc., the Academy of American Poets, and the Society of the Muse of the Southwest (SOMOS).

www.ingramcontent.com/pod-product-compliance
Lightning Source LLC
Chambersburg PA
CBHW022124090426
4274 3CB00008B/999